First World War
and Army of Occupation
War Diary
France, Belgium and Germany

17 DIVISION
Divisional Troops
'A' Squadron Yorkshire Dragoons
28 March 1915 - 15 May 1916

WO95/1991/1

The Naval & Military Press Ltd
www.nmarchive.com
Published in association with The National Archives

Published by

The Naval & Military Press Ltd

Unit 10 Ridgewood Industrial Park,

Uckfield, East Sussex,

TN22 5QE England

Tel: +44 (0) 1825 749494

www.naval-military-press.com

www.nmarchive.com

This diary has been reprinted in facsimile from the original. Any imperfections are inevitably reproduced and the quality may fall short of modern type and cartographic standards.

© Crown Copyright
Images reproduced by permission of The National Archives, London, England, 2015.

Contents

Document type	Place/Title	Date From	Date To
Heading	WO95/1991/1		
Heading	17th Division "A" Sqdn Yorkshire Dragoons Jly 1915-May 1916 To 2 Corps		
Heading	17th Division "A" Squadron Yorkshire Dragoons Vol. I 15-31.7.15. 171/6196		
Heading	War Diary Of "A" Squadron I.O. Yorkshire Dragons. From 15/7/15 to 31/7/15 (Volume 1)		
War Diary	Winchester	15/07/1915	15/07/1915
War Diary	Southampton	15/07/1915	15/07/1915
War Diary	Havre	16/07/1915	16/07/1915
War Diary	Lumbres	17/07/1915	17/07/1915
War Diary	Esquerdes	18/07/1915	18/07/1915
War Diary	Renescure	19/07/1915	19/07/1915
War Diary	Terdeghem	20/07/1915	30/07/1915
War Diary	Boeschepe	31/07/1915	31/07/1915
Heading	17th Division "A" Squadron Yorkshire Dragoons Vol II From 1-31.8.15 121/6607		
Heading	War Diary Of "A" Squadron 1/1st Yorkshire Dragoons 17th Division From 1st Aug. To 31st Aug. 1915 Vol. 2		
War Diary	Boeschepe	01/08/1915	31/08/1915
Heading	17th Division "A" Squadron Yorkshire Dragoons Vol. III Sep 15 121/6992		
Heading	War Diary Of "A" Squadron Q.O. Yorkshire Dragoons 17th Division From 1st Sept.-30 Sept. 1915		
War Diary	Boeschepe	01/09/1915	30/09/1915
War Diary	17th Division "A" Squadron Yorkshire Dragoons Vol. 4 Oct 15 121/7592		
Heading	War Diary Of A Squadron Q.O. Yorkshire Dragoons 17th Division October 1915		
War Diary	Boeschepe	01/10/1915	19/10/1915
War Diary	Winnezeele	20/10/1915	22/10/1915
War Diary	Near Poperinghe	23/10/1915	31/10/1915
Heading	17th Division A Of Yorkshire Dragoons Vol. 5.121/7635 Nov 15		
Heading	War Diary Of (Q.O.) Yorkshire Dragoons A. Sqd. From Nov 1st To Nov 30th 1915 Volume. 5		
War Diary	Lissenhoek	01/11/1915	03/11/1915
War Diary	2 In W. of Poperinghe	04/11/1915	30/11/1915
Heading	17th Div "A" Sq. Yorkshire Dgns Vol 6 121/7931		
Heading	War Diary Of A Sqd Yorkshire Dragoons From 1/12/15 To 31/12/15 Volume 6		
War Diary	2 M.W. Of Poperinghe	01/12/1915	31/12/1915
Heading	War Diary A And Yorkshire Dragoons From Jan 1st To Feb 29th 1916 Vol VIII & IX		
War Diary	2 Miles Next Of Poperinghe	01/01/1916	06/01/1916
War Diary	Arneke	07/01/1916	07/01/1916
War Diary	Salperwick	08/01/1916	07/02/1916
War Diary	Boeschepe	09/02/1916	29/02/1916
Heading	War Diary Of A. Squad Q.O. Yorkshire Dragoons From March 1st 1916 To March 31/16 Volume 9		

War Diary	Boeschepe	01/03/1916	11/03/1916
War Diary	Noote Boom	12/03/1916	24/03/1916
War Diary	Renescure Alquines	25/03/1916	27/03/1916
War Diary	Alquines	28/03/1915	31/03/1915
Heading	War Diary of A. Sqd Yorkshire Dragoons From April 1st 1916 To April 30th 1916 Volume 10		
War Diary	Alquines	01/04/1916	08/04/1916
War Diary	Le Nieppe	09/04/1916	09/04/1916
War Diary	Noote Boom	10/04/1916	30/04/1916
Heading	War Diary (Original) Of A Squad Yorkshire Dragoons. From 1-5-16 To 14-5-16 A. Squad Yorkshire Dragoons Vol 11		
War Diary	Noote Boom	01/05/1916	10/05/1916
War Diary	Hazebrouck	10/05/1916	15/05/1916

VP Sales (© 1991)

17TH DIVISION

'A' SQDN YORKSHIRE DRAGOONS

JLY 1915 - MAY 1916.

To 2 CORPS

17TH DIVISION

14th Division

"A" Squadron Yorkshire Dragoons.

Vol. I. 1.5.15 — 31.7.15.

18 mag '16

Confidential

War Diary
of
"A" Squadron Q.O. Yorkshire Dragoons

from 15/7/15 to 31/7/15

(Volume 1)

Army Form C. 2118.

WAR DIARY
or
INTELLIGENCE SUMMARY.
(Erase heading not required.)

Instructions regarding War Diaries and Intelligence Summaries are contained in F. S. Regs., Part II. and the Staff Manual respectively. Title pages will be prepared in manuscript.

Place	Date	Hour	Summary of Events and Information	Remarks and references to Appendices
WINCHESTER	15/7/15	7 A.M.	Left PITT CORNER CAMP and marched to SOUTHAMPTON. Arrived 11 A.M.	
SOUTHAMPTON	"	11.30 A.D.	Embarked on Transport H.M.T. HUANCHACO.	
"	"	5 P.M.	Sailed. Calm passage, weather fine.	
HAVRE	16/7/15	11 A.M.	Disembarked. Remained in docks all the afternoon. Heavy rain.	
"	"	10.30 P.M.	Left by train.	
LUMBRES	17/7/15	5 P.M.	Detrained - Marched to billets in ESQUERDES. Weather fair.	
ESQUERDES	18/7/15	10.30 A.M.	Left by road for RENESCURE. Arrived 2 P.M. Billets in a farm. Weather fine.	
RENESCURE	19/7/15	10.30 A.M.	Left by road for TERDEGHEM. Arrived 1 P.M. Weather fine. Squadron billeted in one farm. Horses picketed out; water supply poor.	
TERDEGHEM	20/7/15		Weather fine.	
"	21/7/15		Weather fine. A remount drawn at SOUTHAMPTON died of pneumonia.	
"	22/7/15		Fine morning, wet afternoon. Squadron training.	
"	23/7/15		Heavy rain last night. Fine to-day. Squadron training.	
"	24/7/15		Wet morning. Squadron Training.	
"	25/7/15		Sunday. Hailstorm during morning. Afternoon fine.	
"	26/7/15		Fine. Squadron Training.	

Patrick Boyle

Army Form C. 2118.

WAR DIARY
or
INTELLIGENCE SUMMARY.
(Erase heading not required.)

Place	Date	Hour	Summary of Events and Information	Remarks and references to Appendices
TERDEGHEM	27/7/15		Squadron Training. Fine.	
	28/7/15		Squadron Training. Fine.	
	29/7/15		Squadron Training. Fine. One Sergt. & 8 men sent to H.Q. as police.	
	30/7/15 11 A.M.	Left TERDEGHEM and marched to BOESCHEPE. Horse lines in field on POPERINGHE road. Fine & hot. One horse left sick on the road.	
BOESCHEPE	31/7/15		Commenced training field & farm adjoining. Water good for watering horses (pond); all water for drinking has to be fetched 1½ miles and has to be boiled.	

P. [signature]

14th Division

H 121/6607

"A" Squadron Yorkshire Dragoons
Vol: II

From 1 – 31. 8. 15

Confidential

War Diary
of
'A' Squadron 1/1st Yorkshire Dragoons
17th Division

from 1st Aug. to 31st Aug. 1915

vol. 2

Army Form C. 2118.

WAR DIARY
or
INTELLIGENCE SUMMARY.
(Erase heading not required.)

Instructions regarding War Diaries and Intelligence Summaries are contained in F. S. Regs., Part II. and the Staff Manual respectively. Title pages will be prepared in manuscript.

Place	Date	Hour	Summary of Events and Information	Remarks and references to Appendices
BOESCHEPE	1/8/15		Sunday – Church Parade 10 A.M. conducted by R.C. We have left behind on 30/7/15 Bed. training etc.	
"	2/8/15		"	
"	3/8/15		"	
"	4/8/15		"	
"	5/8/15		"	
"	6/8/15		"	
"	7/8/15		"	
"	8/8/15		Sunday. Church Parade 9.30 A.M. conducted by Chaplain 14th Canadians. Weather showery.	
"	9/8/15		Draining of farm building finished.	
"	10/8/15		Very hot. Commenced making new washing place for horse ½ mile away.	
"	11/8/15		Extra. Potato out 5-7 A.M. looking for spies.	
"	12/8/15		New watering place completed. Hot.	
"	13/8/15		Wet afternoon. Lee H. Col Wm Arthur appointed Salvage Officer for Division to collect arms ammunition etc	

WAR DIARY or INTELLIGENCE SUMMARY.

Army Form C. 2118.

(Erase heading not required.)

Instructions regarding War Diaries and Intelligence Summaries are contained in F. S. Regs., Part II. and the Staff Manual respectively. Title pages will be prepared in manuscript.

Place	Date	Hour	Summary of Events and Information	Remarks and references to Appendices
BOESCHEPE	14/8/15		Fine.	
	15/8/15		Showery during morning. Church Parade. Reunion of Officers 97th Regiment at Regimental H.Q. 37th Division: 17 Officers present.	
	16/8/15		2/Lt. Shepherd & 16 N.C.O's men left for H.Q. 5th Corps to be under orders of Camp Commandant.	
	17/8/15		Fine. Preparing men's billet for winter.	
	18/8/15		"	
	19/8/15		"	
	20/8/15		"	
	21/8/15		Heavy rain in morning.	
	22/8/15		Church Parade with D.A.C. Fine. Our watering arrangements have been adopted by 5th Corps as standard pattern.	
	23/8/15		Work on billets.	
	24/8/15		Hot. Work on billets.	
	25/8/15		Hot. Instructed by 5th Corps to build a model hut.	
	26/8/15		Hot. Work on billets.	

T2134. Wt. W708—776. 500000. 4/15. Sir J. C. & S.

Army Form C. 2118.

WAR DIARY
or
INTELLIGENCE SUMMARY.
(Erase heading not required.)

Instructions regarding War Diaries and Intelligence Summaries are contained in F. S. Regs., Part II. and the Staff Manual respectively. Title pages will be prepared in manuscript.

Place	Date	Hour	Summary of Events and Information	Remarks and references to Appendices
BOESCHEPE	27/4/16		4.T. 2/Lt Colman & 73 men left for Clairmarais for woodcutting. Pollu hut commenced.	
	28/4/16		H.T. Stables for winter commenced.	
	29/4/16		Sunday. Church Parade with D.A.C. Much rain.	
	30/4/16		Some rain. Much colder.	
	3/5/16		13 N.C.O. & men attached to A.P.M. 2nd Corps.	

P.H. Steed MAJOR.
COMDG. "A" SQDN. 2OYR

17th Division

121/6994

"A" Squadron Yorkshire Dragoons
Vol: III

Sept. 15

Confidential
War diary
of
"A" Squadron. R.O. Yorkshire Dragoons
17th Division

From 1 Sept. — 30 Sept. 1915

Army Form C. 2118.

WAR DIARY
or
INTELLIGENCE SUMMARY.
(Erase heading not required.)

Instructions regarding War Diaries and Intelligence Summaries are contained in F. S. Regs., Part II. and the Staff Manual respectively. Title pages will be prepared in manuscript.

Place	Date	Hour	Summary of Events and Information	Remarks and references to Appendices
BOESCHEPE	1/9/15		Work on stables and huts. Fine.	
	2/9/15		Ditto	
	3/9/15		Heavy rain all day.	
	4/9/15		Some rain. Work on stables and huts.	
	5/9/15		Sunday. Rained heavily all night. Fine day. Church Parade in hospital.	
	6/9/15		Fine. Work on stables & huts.	
	7/9/15		Fine & hot. Ditto. Began thatching stable roofs.	
	8/9/15		Ditto	
	9/9/15		Ditto	
	10/9/15		Cooler & still fine. Work continued.	
	11/9/15		Fine. Work continued.	
	12/9/15		Sunday. Church Parade. Fine.	
	13/9/15		Fine. Work continued. 6 men returned from Wooltorton's Party.	
	14/9/15		Ditto	
	15/9/15		Ditto	
	16/9/15		Ditto	

Army Form C. 2118.

WAR DIARY
or
INTELLIGENCE SUMMARY.
(Erase heading not required.)

Instructions regarding War Diaries and Intelligence Summaries are contained in F. S. Regs., Part II. and the Staff Manual respectively. Title pages will be prepared in manuscript.

10

Place	Date	Hour	Summary of Events and Information	Remarks and references to Appendices
BOESCHEPE	17/5/15		Fine. Work continued.	
	18/5/15		Do.	
	19/5/15		Sunday. Fine.	
	20/5/15		Fine. Work continued.	
	21/5/15		do. "	
	22/5/15		do. "	
	23/5/15		do. "	
	24/5/15		do. "	
	25/5/15		Some rain.	
	26/5/15		Sunday. Church Parade in Hospital. Fine. Work continued. 13 men returned from A.P.M. 2nd Corps.	
	27/5/15		Fine. Work continued. Wet night.	
	28/5/15		Wet all day.	
	29/5/15		Fine - Wet night.	
	30/5/15		Work completed up to date. B. Ults Recon. consist of a large barn, and a loft above the	

WAR DIARY
or
INTELLIGENCE SUMMARY.
(Erase heading not required.)

Army Form C. 2118.

Place	Date	Hour	Summary of Events and Information	Remarks and references to Appendices
			Farmhouse. The partitions in the barn have been repaired with wattle and mud and the walls repaired. There are 3 rooms. Bunks have been erected of left poles and racks with hurdles and in the loft. A brick floor has been put down in one room of the barn. (Covered) washing accommodation has been provided. All this work is now completed. There is accommodation for all the men. Stables. Two stables have been erected of left poles, thatched with straw. One of these is now completed. Four proposed to make standings of sand. Hut. A wattle hut has been built of wattle and brick earth with a thatched roof. This was built on the instructions of the A.D.M.S. 5th Corps. All the above work has been done to plans made by Captain Brooks and under his direction. With the exception of the thatching, which has been done by civilian labour, all the work has been carried out by men of the Brigade. — [signature]	

121/75qr

17th Hussars

"A" Squadron Yorkshire Dyno"
Vol 4
Oct 15

K

Confidential

War Diary
of
A Squadron. 2.0. Yorkshire Dragoons
17th Division

October 1915

Army Form C. 2118.

13

WAR DIARY
or
INTELLIGENCE SUMMARY.
(Erase heading not required.)

Instructions regarding War Diaries and Intelligence Summaries are contained in F.S. Regs., Part II. and the Staff Manual respectively. Title pages will be prepared in manuscript.

Place	Date	Hour	Summary of Events and Information	Remarks and references to Appendices
BOESCHEPE	1/10/15		Strength of Squadron - 6 Officers, 132 other ranks, 136 horses, 12 mules. Fine. Work on stables continued.	
	2/10/15		Fine. L.B.	
	3/10/15		2nd Sunday. 2nd Church Parade.	
	4/10/15		Horses moved into new stables. Received orders that the division is to move. Midnight.	
	5/10/15			
	6/10/15		Lt. Stafford and detachment returned from Corps Grenadiers, 5th Corps.	
	7/10/15			
	8/10/15		Two men sent to Base Hospital this week owing to sickness.	
	9/10/15		Sunday	
	10/10/15		Began Course of Training of N.C.O's. men in working by map.	
	11/10/15		Training - 2/Lt Calnan & 7 men returned from Dooscutting Party.	
	12/10/15		Training	
	13/10/15		Training	

WAR DIARY
or
INTELLIGENCE SUMMARY.
(Erase heading not required.)

Army Form C. 2118.

Place	Date	Hour	Summary of Events and Information	Remarks and references to Appendices
BOESCHEPE	14/10/15		Training.	
	15/10/15		Training.	
	16/10/15		2/Lt Sir D.B. Austin appointed temporary A.D.C. to G.O.C. 17th Division.	
	17/10/15		Sunday	
	18/10/15		Received orders to vacate billets owing to their being required by 24th Division, & to move to WINNEZEELE.	
	19/10/15		Left BOESCHEPE 10 A.M. and marched to WINNEZEELE. Billeted in one farm 1/2 mile W of village. Horses picketed out. Scarcity of water. Weather very fine.	
WINNEZEELE	20/10/15		Very fine. Training in map reading &c.	
	21/10/15		Left WINNEZEELE 4 A.M. marched to billets N. North Just Horse (3rd Division) 1 mile S.W. of POPERINGHE.	
Nr POPERINGHE	23/10/15		Work on huts & little has been done to prepare this camp for winter use	
"	24/10/15		Sunday. Work on huts etc.	
	25/10/15		Wet all day	

Army Form C. 2118.

15

WAR DIARY
or
INTELLIGENCE SUMMARY.
(Erase heading not required.)

Place	Date	Hour	Summary of Events and Information	Remarks and references to Appendices
PIPERIDGE	26/9/15		Fine generally. Some rain.	
"	27/9/15		Four men went to take part in parade at RENINGHELST inspection by H.M. the King. Mostly wet. Mud very bad in camp and roads leading to it.	
"	28/9/15		Heavy rain	
"	29/10/15		Fine mostly. Work continued	
"	30/10/15		Fine mostly. "	
"	3/10/15		Sunday. Heavy rain	

MAJOR.
COMDG. "A" SQDN. Q.O.Y.D.

Adj: Yokohii Styr
tot: 5

12/7635

17th Division

Nov 15

Confidential

War Diary of

(Q.O.) YORKSHIRE DRAGOONS. A. Sqn.

From Nov 1st. to Nov 30th 1915

Volume 5.

P.J. Smith
MAJOR.
COMDG. "A" SQDN. Q.O.Y.D.
1st Division

WAR DIARY or INTELLIGENCE SUMMARY

Army Form C. 2118.

Place	Date	Hour	Summary of Events and Information	Remarks and references to Appendices
LISSENTHOEK	1/10/15		Strength 7 Squadron 6 Officers, 126 other ranks. Heavy rain. Camp knee-deep in mud.	
	2/10/15		Major Smith took over duties of A.P.M. 27th Divn Dis for a week. Heavy rain. Orders to move next day, owing to this being remain in 9th Divn Area.	
	3/10/15		Left camp at noon, marched to new camp 2 miles W. of POPERINGHE. Borrowed 3 wagons from D.A.C. and 4 from A.S.C. & transported Lufbery material. New camp on higher ground with good water having to lift. Some men in a barn the remainder under canvas. No standings for horses. Showery.	
2m W of POPERINGHE	4/10/15		Began making new huts for men, water troughs etc. Fine.	
	5/10/15		Work continued. Some rain.	
	6/10/15		Work continued. Fine.	
	7/10/15		Sunday.	
	8/10/15		Work continued. Wet.	
	9/10/15		Major Smith returned from duties of A.P.M. Wet.	

WAR DIARY or INTELLIGENCE SUMMARY

Army Form C. 2118.

18

Place	Date	Hour	Summary of Events and Information	Remarks and references to Appendices
2 n. YPRES	9/10/15		Work continued. Wet	
	10/10/15		" Wet	
	11/10/15		Fine	
	12/10/15		Fine	
	13/10/15			
	14/10/15		Sunday. Fine – Church Parade	
	15/10/15		Dug outs not finished.	
	16/10/15		Stables begun. Snow seen	
	17/10/15		Very wet. Hailstorms	
	18/10/15		Enemy aeroplane dropped two bombs close to camp. Wet afternoon	
	19/10/15		Fine part of	
	20/10/15		Fine part of	
	21/10/15		Sunday. Fine morg. Church Parade. Lt Sheppard & 17 men detached to 5th Corps H.Q. water release. 11 Corps tournament all day	
	22/10/15		Hardly frost. Snow thaw	
	23/10/15		Frost	
	24/10/15		Fine. No frost	

Army Form C. 2118.

19

WAR DIARY
or
INTELLIGENCE SUMMARY.
(Erase heading not required.)

Place	Date	Hour	Summary of Events and Information	Remarks and references to Appendices
WEST POPERINGHE	25/4/15		Fine morning. Wet afternoon. 9 men employed on road contest forts under A.P.M. 17th Divn.	
	26/4/15		Snow.	
	27/4/15		Fine Roy.	
	28/4/15		Sunday. Very hard frost. Church Parade. D.S.T.	
	29/4/15		Fine. No frost. Stables, huts & of course and left-pole complete except for floor. All the men now in huts.	

"A" S.F. Yorkshire 8fms.
Vol: 6

121/7931

17/4/57

Confidential

War Diary of

A Sqn Yorkshire Dragoons

From 1/12/15 to 31/12/15

Volume 6

P.J. Stuart MAJOR.
COMDG. "A" SQDN. Q.O.Y.D.
17th Division

WAR DIARY
or
INTELLIGENCE SUMMARY.

Army Form C. 2118.

Place	Date	Hour	Summary of Events and Information	Remarks and references to Appendices
2 A.D. POPERINGHE	1/2/15	—	Strength of Squadron – 6 officers – 125 O.R. 2/Lt. Shepherd and 17 men at Corps H.Q., 2/Lt. Sir Wm Fraser acting A.D.C. to G.O.C. 17th Division, 9 men with A.P.O. 17th Division, 3 men at divisional H.Q. Capt. Brooks and 4 N.C.O's 4 men left for 51st Infantry Brigade to be Instruction work for the Division. Zinc.	
	2/2/15		Work on stables continued. Fine mostly	
	3/2/15		" " " Wet at night.	
	4/2/15		Very wet. Horses brought into stables. Gale at night.	
	5/2/15		Sunday. Fine. Gale at night.	
	6/2/15		Fairly wet.	
	7/2/15		Fine till 4 P.M. then heavy rain –	
	8/2/15		Fine.	
	9/2/15		Very wet all day	
	10/2/15		Wet morning	
	11/2/15		Very wet all day	
	12/2/15		Sunday. Church Parade. Fine morning, wet afternoon.	

Army Form C. 2118.

Instructions regarding War Diaries and Intelligence
Summaries are contained in F. S. Regs., Part II.
and the Staff Manual respectively. Title pages
will be prepared in manuscript.

WAR DIARY
or
INTELLIGENCE SUMMARY.
(Erase heading not required.)

22

Place	Date	Hour	Summary of Events and Information	Remarks and references to Appendices
2nd W.Y POPERINGHE	13/12/15		Fine. Very cold. Lt Colman went to front of CLAIR TAPAIS in road in day	
	14/12/15		Wet.	
	15/12/15		Fine and cold.	
	16/12/15		do	
	17/12/15		Wet afternoon	
	18/12/15		Fine	
	19/12/15		Sunday. 2nd Church Parade. Bombardment of POPERINGHE etc. Gas attack by the front line between YPRES on front of El Caps. YPRES — full of gas for some hours. Capt R.W. Brooke slightly gassed in YPRES — MENIN Road. Attack a complete failure. Heavy bombardment of enemys lines from 5.30 am till dark.	
	20/12/15		Fine	
	21/12/15		Fine	
	22/12/15		Rain	
	23/12/15		Heavy rain in evening	
	24/12/15		Some rain	
	25/12/15		Christmas Day. No training. The men had an excellent Christmas Dinner + a Concert in the Evening in the men's hut	

T2134. Wt. W708—776. 500000. 4/15. Sir J. C. & S.

Army Form C. 2118.

23

WAR DIARY
or
INTELLIGENCE SUMMARY.
(Erase heading not required.)

Instructions regarding War Diaries and Intelligence Summaries are contained in F. S. Regs., Part II. and the Staff Manual respectively. Title pages will be prepared in manuscript.

Place	Date	Hour	Summary of Events and Information	Remarks and references to Appendices
	26/12/15		Sunday. Church Parade. 2pm - Some Kung shows.	
	27/12/15		Lieut. S. P. Clay attached Headquarters 2nd Army for Translation duties. There is now no officer with the Squadron except Major P.S. Marden	
	28/12/15		Routine.	
	29/12/15		Routine.	
	30/12/15		Lieut Colonel W. Mackenzie Smith, O.C. Yorkshire Dragoons, arrived from 37th Division	
	31/12/15		at DOULLENS on tour of inspection of outlying Squadrons (A & C)	

7 Div.
24

Confidential

War Diary
of
"A" Sqn Yorkshire Dragoons

From Jany 1st to Feby 29th 1916.

Vol XIII & IX

Volumes Nos 7 & 8

P.F. Hunt MAJOR.
COMDG. "A" SQDN. Q.O.Y.D.
17th Division

WAR DIARY or INTELLIGENCE SUMMARY

Army Form C. 2118.

25

Place	Date	Hour	Summary of Events and Information	Remarks and references to Appendices
	1916			
2 miles West of POPERINGHE	1.1.16		Routine. Strength 5 Officers 131 other ranks.	
	2.1.16		Routine.	
	3.1.16		Capt. R.W. Boosts and four O.R. rejoined Squadron from H.Q. 51st Infantry Brigade YPRES. Lieut. Col. W. Lackenzie (Brid.) left for PARADIS near MERVILLE to visit C. Squadron.	
	4.1.16		2/Lieut. R. Shepherd and 17 O.R. rejoined Squadron from I Corps H.Q.	
	5.1.16		2/Lieut. R. Shepherd and 2 O.R. left for St MARTIN 1 mile N.W. of St OMER to take over billets in Rest Area from Royal Scots per Squadron. Capt. Galloway, Rey. and Thorpe, Veterinary arrived to take over Command.	
	6.1.16		Squadron marched at 10am to billets at ARNEKE. Horses picketed in the open. Men in barns. Weather fine & cold. road good. distance 18 miles, arrived at 3.30 p.m.	
ARNEKE	7.1.16		834 "B" Sub Went to St OMER Railway Station St MARTIN & SALPERWICK. For billets billeted in disused station, sack tenticloure & bivouacks, horses in loose boxes formerly used as stores, for a sugar beet factory. Officers in various billets of St MARTIN village. Distance 12 miles arrived at 3 P.M. Very hard wintery gale blowing. rain from 11.30 to 2.30. Refilled and rations fresh in wood.	
SALPERWICK	8.1.16		Routine. Cleaning up billets. Individually shooting about only 1/2 to 1 per horse	

T2134. Wt. W706—776. 50C000. 4/15. Sir J.C. & S.

Army Form C. 2118.

26

WAR DIARY
or
INTELLIGENCE SUMMARY.
(Erase heading not required.)

Instructions regarding War Diaries and Intelligence Summaries are contained in F. S. Regs., Part II. and the Staff Manual respectively. Title pages will be prepared in manuscript.

Place	Date	Hour	Summary of Events and Information	Remarks and references to Appendices
	9.1.16		Routine. Stores under orders as much as possible. Equipment	
	6 13.1.16		Inspected & made up. Weather fine	
	14.1.16		Lieut S.C. Long joined Squadron from 37th Division in place J.2nd Lieut C.E. Cadman invalided to England.	
	15.1.16		Horses inspected by A.D.V.S. 17th Division.	
	16.1.16		Routine.	
	17.1.16			
	18.1.16		Division inspected by Major General Sir Herbert Plumer G.O.C. II Army this morning, wet afternoon.	
	19.1.16		Selected gunnery for 100 yds. range. Settled musketry course tomorrow and grouping musketry	
			Preparation, rapid, morning man.	
	20.1.16		Musketry, very windy, wet afternoon	
	21.1.16		Musketry.	
	22.1.16		Musketry	
	23.1.16		Sunday. Church Parade.	
	24.1.16		Musketry	
	25.1.16		Musketry	

Army Form C. 2118.

WAR DIARY
or
INTELLIGENCE SUMMARY.
(Erase heading not required.)

Place	Date	Hour	Summary of Events and Information	Remarks and references to Appendices
	26.1.16		Inspection	
	27.1.16		Tactical Scheme. Squadron thrown forward to reconnoitre an advanced troop to Division Army sounded by 52nd Infantry Brigade	
	28.1.16		Squadron Training.	
	29.1.16		ditto	
	30.1.16		Sunday. Church Parade.	
	31.1.16		Tactical Scheme with 50th Infantry Brigade, Cyclist Company, 12" hole Machine Gun Battery and 79th Brigade R.F.A.	

WAR DIARY or INTELLIGENCE SUMMARY

Army Form C. 2118.

28

Place	Date	Hour	Summary of Events and Information	Remarks and references to Appendices
JALPERWICK	1916			
	1.2.16		Musketry. Instructions in use of Lewis Gun by Lieut H. Sheppard.	
	2.2.16		Musketry. Squadron Training. Lewis gun first on Range.	
	3.2.16		ditto	
	4.2.16		ditto	
	5.2.16		Received orders to relieve 3rd Divisional Cavalry. Lord Kird Horse. 1 officer 5 CTR R.H. arrived to take over. Capt. R.W. Ricards left for BOESCHEPE 6 others ner.	
	6.2.16		Squadron marched at 9.30 a.m. to billets at STEENVOORDE. A hard about 20 miles owen soft roads in billets at 4 p.m. Fine cold day. Horses travelled well. Found transport delayed by soft roads.	
	7.2.16		Marched to billets at BOESCHEPE. The billet in the farms are occupied by the Squadron in August September October 1915. The stables were built of tent poles and thatched roof are still in good order although mud floors are not yet completed, whilst has been forbidden from rain by the roof is still in fair order. The plan of roofing in summer was there is difficulty about getting straw for stand ups; we hoping the ground dry has proved to be a success.	
	8.2.16		One Capt. & 8 others to parade. allotted A.P.M. 17th Division. 1 QUt 6 men took over Salvage Dump.	

T2134. Wt. W708—776. 500000. 4/15. Sir J.C. & S.

Army Form C. 2118.

WAR DIARY
or
INTELLIGENCE SUMMARY.
(Erase heading not required.)

Instructions regarding War Diaries and Intelligence Summaries are contained in F. S. Regs., Part II. and the Staff Manual respectively. Title pages will be prepared in manuscript.

Place	Date	Hour	Summary of Events and Information	Remarks and references to Appendices
BOESCHEPE	9.2.16		Routine.	
	10.2.16		One Sergeant and 12 privates attended A.P.M. 5th Corps.	
	11.2.16		Routine. Enemy of trench & comrades stable above deprun	
	12.2.16		Germans attacked in front of 14th Corps north of Ypres. "Stood by" all night	
	13.2.16		Sunday. Church Parade.	
	14.2.16		German an attack on a front of 17th Division. Enemy reclaimed at midnight & Shortly. West of P. Clay	
			repulsed from Headquarters 2nd Army.	
	15.2.16		Stood by all day until evening of 16th inst.	
	16.2.16		Routine.	
	17.2.16		Routine.	
	18.2.16		Routine.	
	19.2.16		Routine.	
	20.2.16		Sunday. Church Parade	
	21.2.16		Routine. Weather very cold	
	22.2.16		Routine. Heavy fall of snow about front.	
	23.2.16		Routine. Snow afoot	

Army Form C. 2118.

30

WAR DIARY
or
INTELLIGENCE SUMMARY.
(Erase heading not required.)

Instructions regarding War Diaries and Intelligence Summaries are contained in F. S. Regs., Part II. and the Staff Manual respectively. Title pages will be prepared in manuscript.

Place	Date	Hour	Summary of Events and Information	Remarks and references to Appendices
BOESCHEPE	24.2.16		Routine. Hard frost.	
	25.2.16		Routine. Horses tested for glanders with mallein. Heavy fall of snow.	
	26.2.16		Routine. Mallein test satisfactory - no reactor. Hard frost. Frost long caused wet taps memocha have been found to be satisfactory way to get in.	
	27.2.16		Routine Sunday. Church Parade. Thaw.	
	28.2.16		Routine. Thaw.	
	29.2.16		Routine. Fine warm day. Snow all gone.	

A "Yorks Drags" Vol 9

31

Confidential.

War Diary
of
A. Squad. C.O. Yorkshire Dragoons

from March 1st 1916 to March 31/16

Volume 9.

Army Form C. 2118.

32

WAR DIARY
or
INTELLIGENCE SUMMARY.
(Erase heading not required.)

Instructions regarding War Diaries and Intelligence Summaries are contained in F. S. Regs., Part II. and the Staff Manual respectively. Title pages will be prepared in manuscript.

Place	Date	Hour	Summary of Events and Information	Remarks and references to Appendices
BOESCHEPE	1.3.16		Strength 6 Officers 133 other ranks. Ini instruction and at Signalling.	
	2.3.16		Lieut. Long & Sheppard went with 40 men to WOODCOTE HOUSE to take over German prisoners captured in attack on the BLUFF & trenches adjoining. Took over 54 prisoners & marched them over to Divisional Headquarters at RENINGHELST. Lieut. Clay & 25 men went to RENINGHELST & escorted 4 Officers & 103 other ranks prisoners to POPERINGHE Station. Weather fine.	
	3.3.16		Lieut. Long's party arrived back in Camp at 6 a.m. Lieut. Clay & 25 men went to RENINGHELST & escorted 98 prisoners to POPERINGHE. Got back to camp 10 p.m. Very wet night. Rain & snow.	
	4.3.16		Routine. Heavy snow in morning. Ameldin returned from Signal Coy.	
	5.3.16		Sunday. Church Parade. Some snow showers.	
	6.3.16		Routine. Heavy snow during night, early morning. Two orderlies rejoined from Signal Coy. Returned party C.S.M. Roach had Horne (3rd Division) arrived to take over.	
	7.3.16		Routine. Snow.	
	8.3.16		Routine. Heavy snow. Orders to move to II Corps Area.	
	9.3.16		Routine.	
	10.3.16		Routine. Some snow.	
	11.3.16		Rec'd order to billets at WOOTE BOOM in II Corps Area. Area in town reliable men in service transport Coy.	

YORKSHIRE DNS.

Army Form C. 2118.

XVIIth DIVISION

33

WAR DIARY
or
INTELLIGENCE SUMMARY.
(Erase heading not required.)

Place	Date	Hour	Summary of Events and Information	Remarks and references to Appendices
MOOTE BOOM.	12.3.16		Practise trench fire.	
	13.3.16		Reconnaissance of Divisional Area. Fire practice	
	14.3.16		ditto — Lieut Sheppard & 10 men took on Patrol & Scout.	
	15.3.16		— ditto —	
	16.3.16		— ditto —	
	17.3.16		Twenty seven other ranks attached A.P.M. 17th Division for police duty in ARMENTIERES.	
	18.3.16		Route march	
	"		"	
	23.3.16		"	
	24.3.16		6 N.C.Os & men attached to Infantry Brigades for observation duties.	
			The Squadron (less Capt R.W. Brooke, 2/Lt L. Gillum Scott, 4 N.C.Os. at Divnl. H.Q. 8 O.R. attached A.P.M. & 6 O.R. attached Infantry Brigades) left II Corps area for fortnight training and this 2nd Cavalry Division	
			Marched 16 miles to RENESCURE turned into billets. Roads fairly good, made very cold through snow & sleet.	
RENESCURE.	25.3.16		Marched 30 miles to ALQUINES	
ALQUINES.	26.3.16		Inspection of troops by Major General Sir Philip Chetwode G.O.C 2nd Cavalry Division, detailed to 6th Bde cav.	
	27.3.16		Route march of Divisional Squadrons (John Jackson Instr.) Cancelled owing to bad weather (snow)	
			Under G.O.C. 6th Cavalry Division — Very cold wet stormy of snow & rain	

Army Form C. 2118.

34

WAR DIARY
or
INTELLIGENCE SUMMARY.
(Erase heading not required.)

Instructions regarding War Diaries and Intelligence Summaries are contained in F. S. Regs., Part II. and the Staff Manual respectively. Title pages will be prepared in manuscript.

Place	Date	Hour	Summary of Events and Information	Remarks and references to Appendices
ALQUINES	28.3.15		Squadron training. Fine cold	
	29.3.15		— ditto — Fine cold	
	30.3.15		— ditto — Weather turned warmer	
	31.3.15		— ditto — Fine pleasant	

"A" Yorks Drags
Vol 10

Confidential
War Diary
of
A.Sqd. Yorkshire Dragoons

From April 1st 1916 to April 30th 1916

Volume

F. Keighley, Major.
Comdg. "A" Sqdn. Q.O.Y.D.
17th Division

Army Form C. 2118.

36

WAR DIARY
or
INTELLIGENCE SUMMARY.
(Erase heading not required.)

Instructions regarding War Diaries and Intelligence Summaries are contained in F. S. Regs., Part II. and the Staff Manual respectively. Title pages will be prepared in manuscript.

Place	Date	Hour	Summary of Events and Information	Remarks and references to Appendices
ALQUINES	1.4.16		Squadron Training. Weather fine.	
	2.4.16		Sunday	
	3.4.16		Squadron Training. " "	
	5		" " "	
	8.4.16		Squadron Training.	
LE MIEPPE	9.4.16		Marched from Cavalry Division Area. Billeted at LE MIEPPE. March 20 miles. Roads good.	
NOOTE BOOM	10.4.16		Marched to billets at NOOTE BOOM in II Corps Area. March 16 miles. 4 O.R. attached II Corps H.Q.	
			Two Officers (Lieuts CLAY & SHEPPARD) attached 4th Cavalry Brigade for Hotchkiss gun course.	
	11.4.16		26 O.R. attached A.P.M. 9th Division for Permit Control duties.	
	12.4.16		Routine.	
	13.4.16		3 O.R. attached as orderlies to 7th Squadron R.F.C.	
	14.4.16		29 O.R. attached A.P.M. 17th Division.	
	15.4.16		Routine.	
	16.4.16		6 O.R. attached Salvage Corps 17th Division.	
	17.4.16		1 Officer (Lieut LENG) & 4 O.R. attached II Army Machine Gun School for Hotchkiss Gun Course.	
	18.4.16		Routine.	
	19.4.16		Reinforcement. 3 men from No. 5 Base Depot.	

Army Form C. 2118.

WAR DIARY
or
INTELLIGENCE SUMMARY.
(Erase heading not required.)

Place	Date	Hour	Summary of Events and Information	Remarks and references to Appendices
NUTE BOOM	20.4.16		Routine. Instruction in Hotchkiss Rifle.	
	21.4.16		" "	
	22.4.16		" "	
	23.4.16		Easter Sunday. Church Parade.	
	24.4.16		Routine. Instruction in Hotchkiss Rifle.	
	25.4.16		" " Lewis Pistols & attacks in Kings of Enemy Cavalry.	
			Lieutg. N.A.R. reported from US Army hostiles on Patrol	
			2nd Lieut M F B Stephenson joined from R.E. Base Depot	
	26.4.16		2 B.O. R returned from A.P.M. 9th Division	
			R/C Clay proceeded to 8 days leave to Pup Land	
			" under 2nd Lieng; Che Baght & Epl Roulitt	
			Horse destroyed — broken neck	
	27.4.16		" " " under A.R.Eng	
	28.4.16		" " " under A.R.Eng	
			Horse inspected by Vet. O.H. + buried by	
			this unit.	
	29.4.16		" "	

WAR DIARY or INTELLIGENCE SUMMARY

Army Form C. 2118.
38

Place	Date	Hour	Summary of Events and Information	Remarks and references to Appendices
NOOTEBOOM	30-4-16	2 A.M.	Poison Gas drifting from KEMMEL – 10 kilometres distant – Guard (previously posted) warned all billets. Two casualties – Major P.G. Smith & Sergt. Platts whose rooms must have been in the direct path of two separate currents of air leaving the gas. Most of squadron complained of slight effects. Major Smith & Sergt. Platts to hospital, former with high temperature. Contagions arrived at. from this experience show importance of keeping still during passage of gas, & rapid handling of helmet.	
		3 p.m.	Inspection of gas helmets by R. Leng	
		3.15 p.m.	Church parade	

A. Squad
Yorks Drags
Vol 11

XXXII

39

War Diary (Original).

of

A. Squad. Yorkshire Dragoons.

From 1-5-16 To 14-5-16

A P Clark
MAJOR.
COMDG. "A" SQDN. Q.O.Y.D.

Confidential.

WAR DIARY
or
INTELLIGENCE SUMMARY.
(Erase heading not required.)

Army Form C. 2118.

40

Place	Date	Hour	Summary of Events and Information	Remarks and references to Appendices
MOOZE BOOM	1-5-16		Routine - Hotchkiss Gun Class under D'Leng. - Two N.C.O's attached for one day's course 17th Div. Art. for Schools	
	2-5-16		" - " Horse destroyed - broken fetlock	
			" - " Horse buried. Reinforcements -	
			" - " 2.O.R. arrival Major Smith much improved	
	3.5.16		Routine - Hotchkiss Class	
	4.5.16		" "	
	5.5.16		" "	
	6.5.16		Routine - Horse destroyed - broken shoulder.	
	7.5.16		Sunday -	
	8.5.16		Orders to move on 10th to area N. of HAZEBROUCK. Thereon Corps Tugr. also to relieve 9th Div. Potter at STEENWERCK.	
	9.5.16		Sgt Houghton & 27 men went to STEENWERCK.	
			Left MOOTE BOOM 9.30 AM. Reached new billets 12 noon, on	
	10.5.16		HONDEGHEM road, ¾ m. N. of HAZEBROUCK. Horse picketed out.	

R. M. Clark

Army Form C. 2118.

WAR DIARY
or
INTELLIGENCE SUMMARY.
(Erase heading not required.)

Place	Date	Hour	Summary of Events and Information	Remarks and references to Appendices
HAZEBROUCK to	10/5/16		Cpl Clement reports returned from Salvage Dump.	
"	11/5/16		Routine.	
"	12/5/16		Represented Nr. 13 Sqdn. arrived. C Sqdn. led arrived in gets. Very wet night.	
	13/5/16		Rot. weather the day. Routine.	
	14/5/16		Sunday. Lt King (on leave) ordered to report at BISLEY for amm.m. course.	
	15/5/16			

L. P. Clayton

www.ingramcontent.com/pod-product-compliance
Lightning Source LLC
Chambersburg PA
CBHW081455160426
43193CB00013B/2489